Date: 11/09/11

SUPER SMART
INFORMATION
STRATEGIES

INFORMATION
EXPLORER

PUT IT ALL
TOGETHER

by Phyllis Cornwall

CHERRY LAKE PUBLISHING • ANN ARBOR, MICHIGAN

CHERRY LAKE
Publishing

Published in the United States of America
by Cherry Lake Publishing
Ann Arbor, Michigan
www.cherrylakepublishing.com

Content Adviser: Gail Dickinson, PhD,
Associate Professor, Old Dominion University,
Norfolk, Virginia

Book design and illustration: The Design Lab

Photo credits: Cover, ©Blend Images/Alamy; pages 3, 5, 12, 17, 26 left, and
29, ©iStockphoto.com/bluestocking; page 4, ©iStockphoto.com/Yarinca; page
6 top, ©Willierossin/Dreamstime.com; page 6 bottom, ©Monkey Business
Images/Dreamstime.com; page 11, ©iStockphoto.com/KenCanning; page 15,
©iStockphoto.com/Veni; page 23, ©Jinlide/Dreamstime.com; page 26 right,
©iStockphoto.com/jsemeniuk

Library of Congress Cataloging-in-Publication Data
Cornwall, Phyllis.
  Super smart information strategies. Put it all together / by Phyllis
Cornwall.
      p. cm.—(Information explorer)
  Includes bibliographical references and index.
  ISBN-13: 978-1-60279-643-0   ISBN-10: 1-60279-643-2 (lib.bdg.)
  ISBN-13: 978-1-60279-651-5   ISBN-10: 1-60279-651-3 (pbk.)
  1. Report writing—Juvenile literature. I. Title. II. Title: Put it all
together. III. Series
   LB1047.3.C67 2009
   372.13028'1—dc22   2009027806

Cherry Lake Publishing would like to acknowledge the work
of The Partnership for 21st Century Skills. Please visit
www.21stcenturyskills.org for more information.

Printed in the United States of America
Corporate Graphics Inc.
January 2010
CLSP06

A NOTE TO PARENTS AND TEACHERS: Please remind your children how to stay safe online before they do the activities in this book.

A NOTE TO KIDS: Always remember your safety comes first!

Table of Contents

CHAPTER ONE
Gather Your Resources

You've worked hard for weeks. You've searched through print materials and Web sites to find a lot of information. You carefully chose your sources. You've taken notes. "This research project will be great," you remind yourself. But your work is just beginning. Now you must switch from gathering facts and information to presenting it. It is time to put it all together!

Books are just one resource you can use when looking for information.

How do you move from collecting information to sharing it? It's important to stay organized. You will be glad you did! Think of your research and citations as valuable goods. Wouldn't you keep something important in a safe spot? Collect your notes, images, and graphic organizers, such as charts and graphs. Keep them in one place. Store any print resources in a folder or large envelope. Using electronic sources? Create a folder on the computer. Save all your documents there. Storing your sources in these ways makes it much easier for you to find information when you need it.

Consider
THIS

Name your Word documents and folders carefully. Think of labels that help you remember what is in the file. Are you working with a group? Are you all saving your research in the same place? Be extra careful. Add your last name or initials to the file name. Pretend your last name is Flores and you are working on a project about gorillas. You could save a Word document of your notes as GorillasFlores.doc. Everyone will know that the Word document contains your information.

You might work from both a home and school computer. Check with your teacher and parents. Find out if you can store and transport your documents on a flash drive. Or think about posting your research to a collaborative online tool. One option is a wiki. No matter how you choose to store your information, the goal is to stay organized. Find a way that works for you.

USB flash drive
4 Gb

Flash drives are small and portable. They are great for storing information.

If you are working with a group, a wiki may be the best way to share information. Your teacher can help you set up a wiki.

TRY THIS!

Have you ever been caught in the dark when the power went out? Research how to make a blackout supply kit. With the help of your parents, think about items that you should include. Look online for tips about how to stay safe in a blackout. Take notes. Keep your research and list of items organized in a way that works for you. You might use a binder. Now put together the kit. Use a box or container and label it "Blackout Supplies." You might include flashlights, extra batteries, blankets, and bottled water. Keep the binder or folder and kit in a place where everyone can easily reach it. Organizing resources so that they are easy to get to is very important during an emergency. It is just as important to organize your resources and information during a school project!

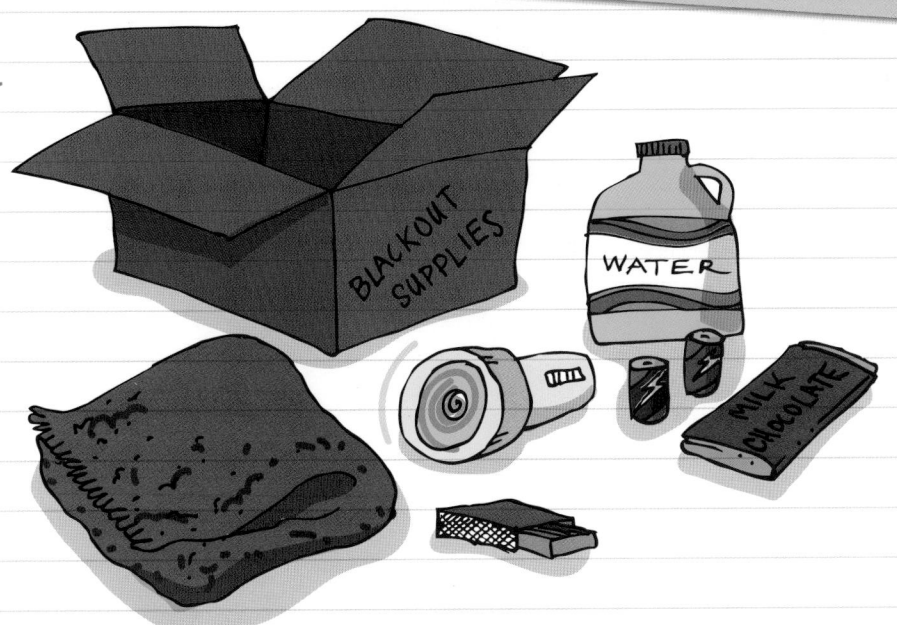

CHAPTER TWO
Sift Your Information

Congratulations! Your information is organized and easy to search through. You are on your way to a successful project. It is a smart idea to recheck the directions of your assignment. Be sure you understand why and how the information is to be shared. Think of the directions as learning goals as you work through all stages of your project. Concentrating on these learning goals will keep you focused.

Imagine you are on the beach. You are sifting through the sand to find shells. Information that helps you reach your goals is like the seashells. The sand represents extra facts and information that don't relate to your topic.

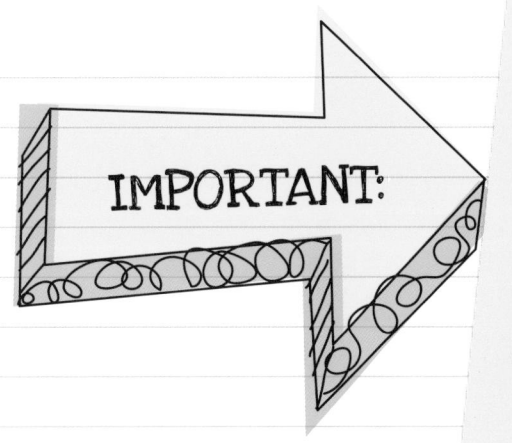

IMPORTANT:

Be sure all your information comes from reliable sources. Reliable sources are usually written by experts and contain current information. You don't want to use incorrect facts or outdated information.

When sifting your information, think about how useful it may be. Take a look at all the items you found. You might have cool pictures, interesting facts, and great interviews. Your job is to look at everything you collected. Then decide if you have what you need to complete your project.

Use these key points to help you sift. Ask if you have enough information to:

- Answer your questions
- Help make decisions
- Help solve a problem
- Teach yourself something new
- Draw conclusions

Sifting through information can be confusing or frustrating. Don't worry. Sometimes, even the best information explorers get stuck. Let's consider some problems you may run into along the way.

Consider the research you gathered as a whole. Are there any gaps in information? Gaps in information are missing pieces. They can cause you to make false conclusions. You do not want to misinform your audience. Pretend you collected data about the reliability of a product. But all of your data covers only a small period of time. With this information, you can't decide if the product will be reliable over a long period of time. Fix gaps by being thorough. Try to think of questions other people might have about your topic. Can you answer all of these questions using the information you have collected? If not, you might need to find more sources.

Can you spot any weaknesses in your information as a whole? If so, you might not have checked enough sources. Consider an article that said you could attract wildlife to your yard by planting wildflowers. You decide to plant some pretty purple wildflowers. But you didn't find out from other sources which flowers would be best. What you planted, unfortunately, is a type of flower that takes over and causes problems for some wildlife. Fix weaknesses by making sure you have enough information from different sources.

Conflicting information includes ideas or facts that do not agree. Pretend you read that you should drink

Where would you look for reliable information about the kinds of plants deer like to eat?

eight glasses of water each day. Your friend shows you another article that says you don't need to drink that much water. Avoid conflicting information by making sure your sources are reliable. What if you find conflicting views in reliable sources? Go ahead and present both sides of the idea.

Misleading information is information that gives a wrong or inaccurate idea about something. Avoid misleading information by investigating ideas that seem too good to be true. Be careful if something seems to be an opinion instead of a fact. Dig deep and collect more research to reach an informed conclusion.

TRY THIS!

Practice your sifting skills. Write a list of 15 words that describe you. Imagine you want to apply to be a safety monitor at your school. Look at the list you wrote. Are there traits you could use to convince your principal that you would be a good safety monitor? Can you use all of the words you wrote? Probably not. Maybe you wrote down that you are both responsible and silly. *Responsible* is a better word than *silly* for your purpose. Do you need to add some more words? Sift the terms that would be best to use. With those terms, write a short paragraph on why you would be a good safety monitor. Do you see how sifting helps you focus your ideas?

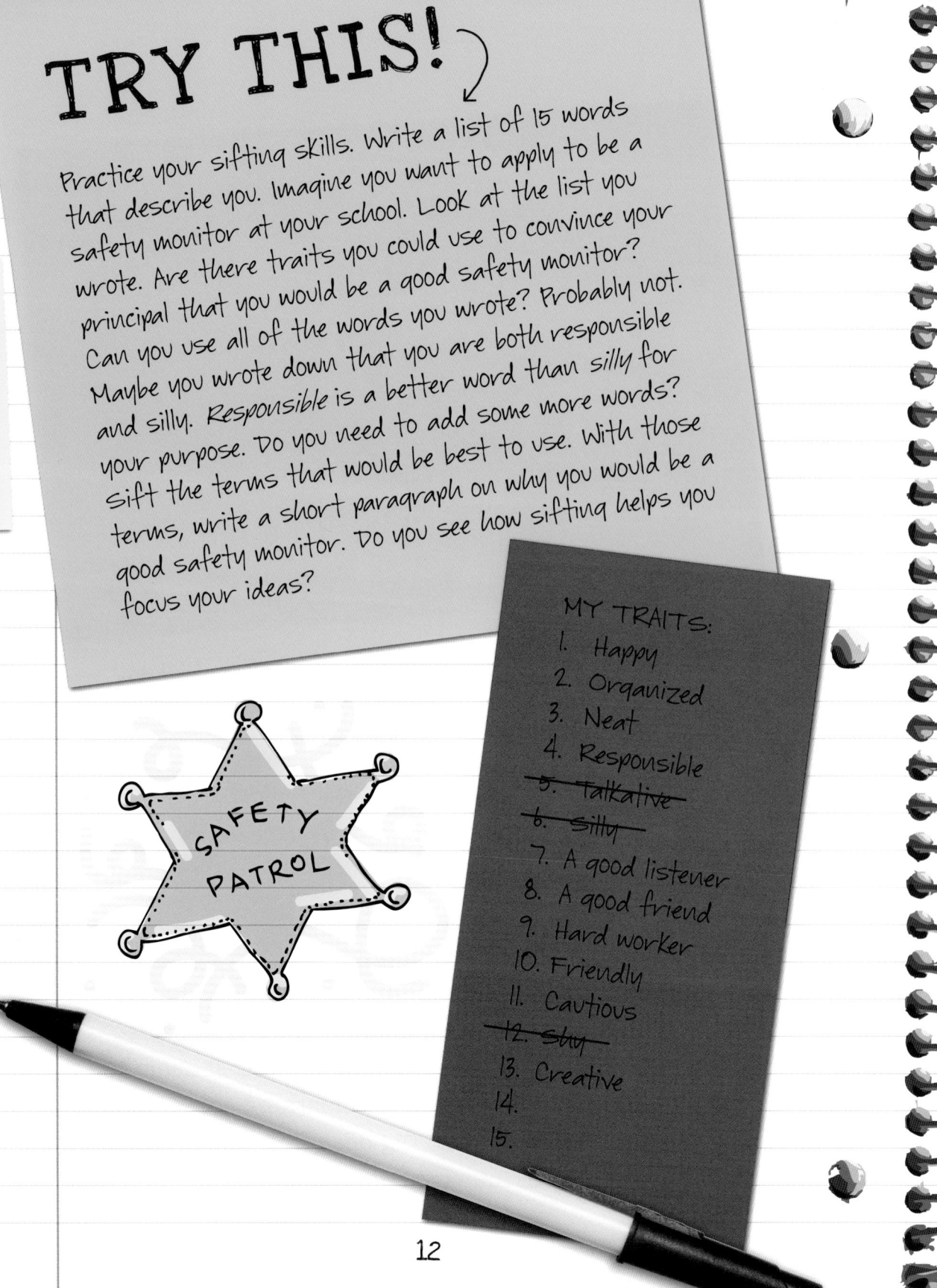

SAFETY PATROL

MY TRAITS:
1. Happy
2. Organized
3. Neat
4. Responsible
5. ~~Talkative~~
6. ~~Silly~~
7. A good listener
8. A good friend
9. Hard worker
10. Friendly
11. Cautious
12. ~~Shy~~
13. Creative
14.
15.

CHAPTER THREE

Organize Your Discoveries

You picked out the good stuff. Now you have piles and files of valuable items. Let's work on making sense out of what you have saved. Organizing information can help you in many ways. You'll get a better idea of what you've found. You may come up with the best ways to use that information, too.

There are many different ways to organize your information. Graphic organizers are useful tools. They can help you collect and arrange your research. They can help you see how different pieces of information fit together.

Charts are one type of graphic organizer. They can help you decide how to develop a project. Putting ideas into rows and columns can help you see all of your options.

Charts can be a great way to organize information.

Animal	Food	Supplies	Hours of care/day
Dog			
Cat			
Goldfish			
Parakeet			

FAMILY PET IDEAS

TRY THIS!

Ready to practice using a graphic organizer? Here is an example of a chart you might use for a project about planning a family vacation:

continued ⟶

stop, wait, don't write in this book! Redraw or make a photocopy of the chart below.

Family Vacation Ideas

LOCATION	HIKING OR OTHER OUTDOOR ACTIVITY	SHOPPING	RESTAURANTS	FAMILY FUN ACTIVITIES
Boston, Massachusetts				
Seattle, Washington				
Traverse City, Michigan				
Atlanta, Georgia				

TRY THIS! (CONTINUED)

1. Redraw or make a photocopy of the chart. Feel free to change the cities or activities.

2. Research information to fill in the rows and columns. Find information about options for outdoor activities in each city. List any famous restaurants or shopping spots. Include other activities that families can do together, too. Ask an adult for permission if you are researching online.

Look at the facts after you've completed the chart. Did using a chart help you organize your info in a useful way?

Another type of graphic organizer is a concept map. A concept map is a special diagram. It helps you see how your ideas fit together. You put ideas in boxes or bubbles and link them with labels and arrows. Concept maps help you visually connect related ideas to your topic. During and after your research, you can build up your map with more facts and connections.

A concept map helps guide your project. Let's say your assignment is to explain a topic related to thunderstorms. The diagram on the following page shows the start of a concept map about thunderstorms. This example might give you the idea to focus your project on the harm thunderstorms can do. You could expand your thoughts using the ideas from the "damage" bubble.

Charts and concept maps are just two types of graphic organizers. There are many others that you might find helpful.

Always ask a teacher or other adult if you have questions.

Ask a librarian, teacher, or other adult to help you find free graphic organizers online. You'll see how fun and useful they can be!

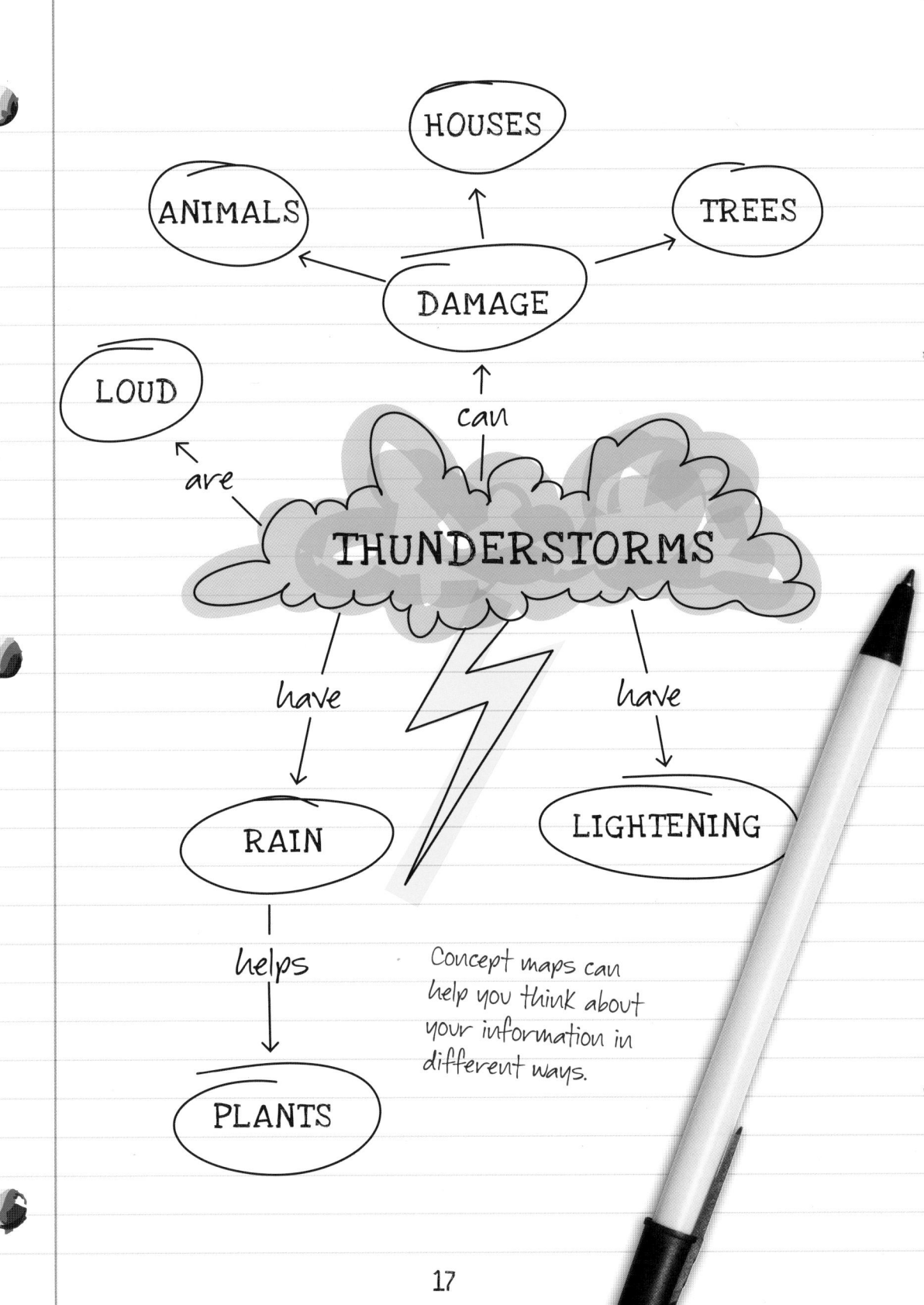

HOUSES

ANIMALS

TREES

DAMAGE

LOUD

can

are

THUNDERSTORMS

have

have

RAIN

LIGHTENING

helps

Concept maps can
help you think about
your information in
different ways.

PLANTS

CHAPTER FOUR
Consider Your Purpose and Audience

Now it is time to take the information you sifted and organized and plan how to put it all together. What's the purpose of your research in the first place? To inform? To persuade? To teach something? To answer questions? Use that purpose to help you put your project together.

Let's say you are a member of the student council. You must all decide on themes for some "school spirit" days. You've researched what had been done in previous years. You've gathered ideas from other students. All the council members have discussed the ideas and voted on the choices. The decisions were made. Now the information needs to be shared with the whole school. How can that be done?

When you want to inform someone, you need to communicate the important facts. Everyone doesn't need to know all the choices that were discussed. They need to know what was chosen. When you inform someone, weed out the unimportant details. Present the facts in ways that are easy to remember. Spirit day themes

Your idea can be presented in many ways. A button may be one way to promote school pride.

could be shared through posters. They could also be announced on your school broadcasting system. Or they could be listed on your school Web site.

Now imagine you're at your friend's house. She has a new pet chinchilla. You would love to have one, too. Then, you remember you have that assignment from Mr. Lamb. You must write a persuasive paper. You need to pick a topic that you feel strongly about. You also need to choose your audience. Aha! You have the

You may think chinchillas are cute, but your mom may think they look like mice. Convincing her may take more than pictures!

perfect topic: owning a chinchilla. You've also thought of the perfect audience: your parents. Your assignment can help you win over your parents. Showing them some well-researched information about pet chinchillas just might convince them.

What does it mean to persuade someone? You convince that person to believe or do something. You want to hook her with your ideas. You also want to present your claim in an appealing way. Try multimedia presentations. They allow you to combine the power of pictures, sounds, and words.

Now pretend that you've been researching the art of origami. Your assignment is to explain how to make an origami bird. How could you do that? A step-by-step demonstration is a good idea. Try making a video of yourself showing how to make the origami bird. Can't find available video equipment? Take photos or draw pictures of each step. Then create a slide show.

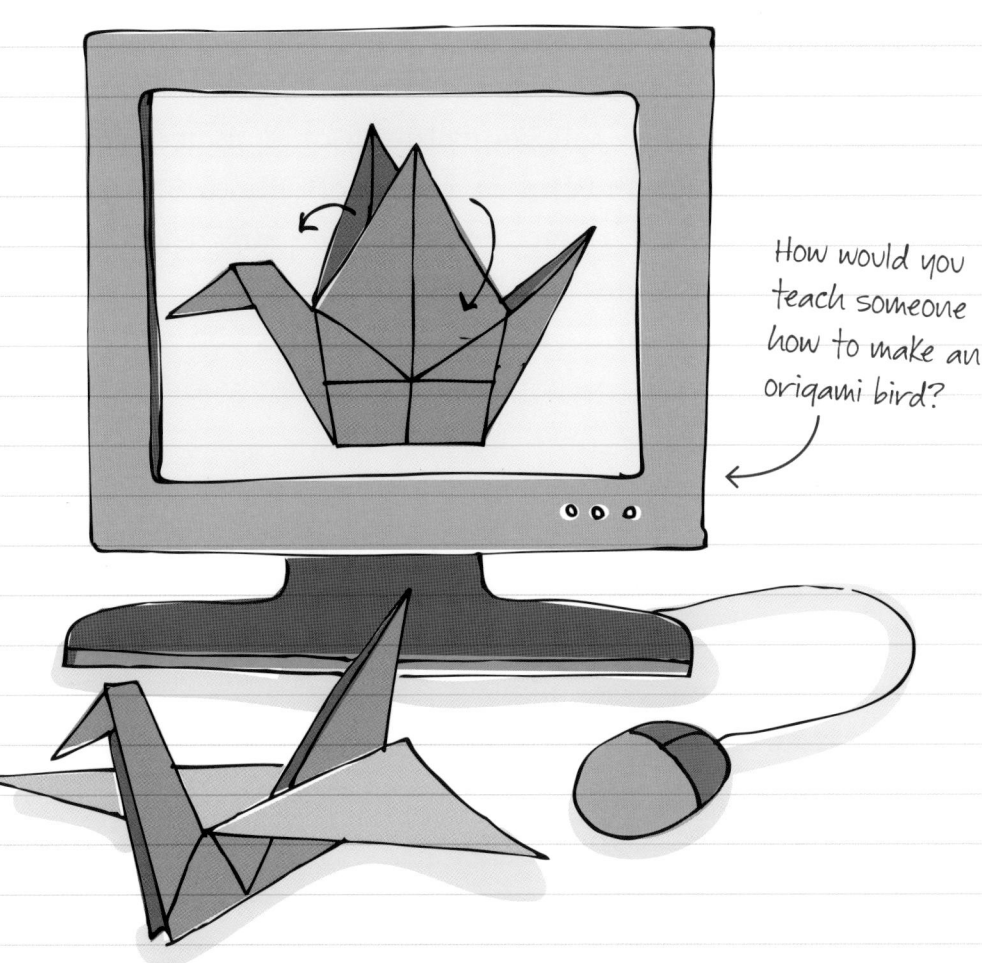

How would you teach someone how to make an origami bird?

What would your life be like if you lived at another time? How would it be different from the present? There will be times when your assignment is to answer specific questions such as these. How can you present your answers? Let's say you found some photos of objects or documents from the time period. Maybe you want to display them along with photos from your own life. This is a great way to show people the differences and similarities of the two time periods. You may decide to choose a program that allows you to import pictures to tell your story. Some choices might be Microsoft PowerPoint or Microsoft Photo Story. Ask a media specialist or your teacher for suggestions for other programs you could use.

Clearly, it is important to know why you are doing research. It's also important to consider your audience.

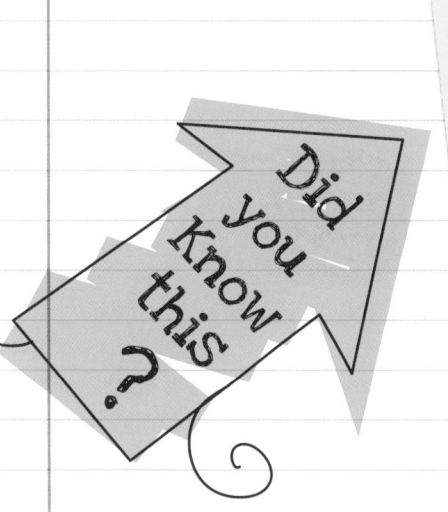
Did you Know this?

Photo Story is a free download from Microsoft. With this program, you can put together slideshows of photographs. Just remember to ask your parents before downloading anything!

You are part of an audience whenever you watch a movie, dance recital, or sports event. An audience listens or watches. Your project or presentation will have an audience. It could be one person or many people. Your audience could be your best friend, your grandmother, or a five-year-old child. If you are working on a project for school, your teacher is an important member of your audience. Knowing who is listening, reading, or watching can help you decide how to get your message across.

Your audience helps determine the content and design of your project. What are members of your audience interested in? What words will they recognize? Keep these ideas in mind.

Who is the audience for a science fair project?

TRY THIS!

Do you like to play a certain sport or do a certain craft? Pretend you are going to teach that activity to a kindergartener, a friend your age, and your teacher. Create three different presentations.

CONSIDER THE FOLLOWING ABOUT YOUR AUDIENCE:

- What does he or she already know about the activity?
- What can he or she physically do?
- How does he or she learn best? Visually? A different way?
- Can he or she easily understand your written or spoken messages?
- How do different audiences affect your approach to the topic?

Do you like baseball? How would you teach someone else about the game?

CHAPTER FIVE
Present Your Discoveries

Now you are ready to dazzle everyone. Your project will really make your audience think. Were you given presentation guidelines by your teacher? Were you told to present in a certain format? Maybe you must make a poster or write a report. Check the instructions of your assignment once more to make sure you are using the right format. Choose designs that strengthen your message, but do not overshadow it.

Programs for creating presentations have many features. Some have great animations and sound clips. Choose such extras very carefully. You don't want to develop a project that looks great but doesn't say much. Your audience—especially your teacher—will notice. A flashy project without a strong base of information won't get you a good grade.

Consider THIS

TRY THIS!

Go on a hunt. Find how information is shared all around you. Bring a camera, notebook, and pencil. See how information is shared about products, rules, or ideas. Watch commercials on television. Study signs you see outside. Examine different rooms you visit at your school. Are there posters or displays of another student's work? Your goal is to find examples of good ways to share information. Take photos of those examples.

continued ⟶

TRY THIS! (CONTINUED)

On your hunt, record your answers to these questions in your notebook:

1. What is the purpose of the information?
2. What grabs your attention?
3. What surprises you?
4. What makes you wonder?
5. What can you improve?
6. Why do you think the message was communicated in this way?
7. How does the design get the message across?

Take notes and pictures of presentations that you find interesting.

Can you use these ideas in ways that work for you? Don't copy someone else's design. Take the good ideas and adapt them for your project.

Do you want to present your information in a speech? Get creative. Try a debate, puppet show, or video talk show. Do you want to produce a product? How about a brochure, poster, game, or cartoon? If you want to make a multimedia project, consider using a program such as PowerPoint.

Remember to think carefully about your format. Will the way you present your information work for your message and audience? Can you use it to cover all your learning goals?

Don't forget to give credit to your sources. You cannot claim someone else's words, ideas, pictures, or any other information as your own. Ask your teacher to help you figure out how to credit different sources.

You took your discoveries and determined what was useful. You organized your thoughts. You expressed your message in an interesting and effective way. You kept your learning goals in mind. You remembered your audience. Congratulations on a successful project. With practice, you'll get better and better at putting it all together. So keep at it. You'll be an expert information explorer in no time!

REPORT CARD

Presentation and topic:
Puppet show about recycling
presented to 4th and 5th grade

Research	A
Organization	A
Presentation	A+
Audience appeal	A

Take a moment for some self-assessment. Did you do a good job of putting it all together? Do you need to work on sifting the useful information from the extra details? Maybe you could work on organizing research and information in ways that are more useful. Learning to spot your weaknesses is a good thing. It is the first step toward improving your skills!

Glossary

citations (sye-TAY-shuhnz) acts or instances of giving credit to the source of a fact, quote, or other information

collaborative (kuh-LAB-uh-ruh-tiv) having to do with working together to do something

columns (KOL-uhmz) setups of information that run up and down in a chart, table, or on a printed page

concept map (KON-sept MAP) a diagram with boxes and arrows that shows relationships between ideas

content (KON-tent) the information or topics in a written work, speech, or project

flash drive (FLASH DRIVE) a small, portable storage device used to save files and information

format (FOR-mat) the arrangement, organization, or style of something

graphic organizers (GRAF-ik OR-guh-nye-zurz) visual representations that help organize information and show relationships between ideas

rows (ROHZ) setups of information that run side to side in a chart or table

self-assessment (self-uh-SESS-muhnt) the process of rating your progress, strengths, and weaknesses and determining points that need improvement or changes you can make

sifting (SIF-teeng) separating out or sorting through in order to find something useful

wiki (WI-kee) a Web site that allows users to add and edit content and information

Find Out More

BOOKS

Bullard, Lisa. *Ace Your Oral or Multimedia Presentation*. Berkeley
    Heights, NJ: Enslow Publishers, 2009.

Faundez, Anne. *How to Write Reports*. Laguna Hills, CA: QEB
    Publishing, Inc., 2007.

Orr, Tamra B. *Extraordinary Research Projects*. New York: Franklin
    Watts, 2006.

WEB SITES

BBC—Speaking Skills

www.bbc.co.uk/schools/ks3bitesize/english/speaking_listening/speak_3.shtml

Giving an oral presentation? Read advice for a successful speech.

Microsoft Photo Story 3 for Windows—Make Show-n-tell Cool Again

www.microsoft.com/windowsxp/using/digitalphotography/photostory/default.mspx

Ask an adult to help you download this program and create your own photo slideshows.

TIME For Kids—Homework Helper: Research Paper

www.timeforkids.com/TFK/kids/hh/writeideas/articles/0,28372,606651,00.html

Find helpful tips for putting together a research paper.

Index

About the Author

Phyllis Cornwall is an elementary media specialist. She lives in Michigan with her husband, Bryan, and their five cats. She is the proud mother of Dan, Lydia, and Ben, and the proud stepmother of Amanda and Tessa. Phyllis is also the proud mother-in-law of Travis. She loves being an information explorer.